I0211292

SUMMER OF HAROLD

A TRIO OF PLAYS FOR TWO ACTORS

HILARY BELL

CURRENCY PRESS
The performing arts publisher

ENS
THEATRE E
MB
ML E

CURRENT THEATRE SERIES

First published in 2023
by Currency Press
Gadigal Land, PO Box 2287 Strawberry Hills, NSW, 2012, Australia
enquiries@currency.com.au
www.currency.com.au

in association with Ensemble Theatre

Copyright: *Summer of Harold* © Hilary Bell, 2023.

COPYING FOR EDUCATIONAL PURPOSES

The Australian *Copyright Act 1968* [Act] allows a maximum of one chapter or 10% of this book, whichever is the greater, to be copied by any educational institution for its educational purposes provided that that educational institution [or the body that administers it] has given a remuneration notice to Copyright Agency [CA] under the Act.

For details of the CA licence for educational institutions contact CA, 12 / 66 Goulburn Street, Sydney, NSW, 2000; tel: within Australia 1800 066 844 toll free; outside Australia 61 2 9394 7600; fax: 61 2 9394 7601; email: memberservices@copyright.com.au

COPYING FOR OTHER PURPOSES

Except as permitted under the Act, for example a fair dealing for the purposes of study, research, criticism or review, no part of this book may be reproduced, stored in a retrieval system, or transmitted in any form or by any means without prior written permission. All enquiries should be made to the publisher at the address above.

Any performance or public reading of *Summer of Harold* is forbidden unless a licence has been received from the author or the author's agent. The purchase of this book in no way gives the purchaser the right to perform the play in public, whether by means of a staged production or a reading. All applications for public performance should be addressed to the author c /- RGM, info@rgm.com.au, phone +61 2 9281 3911.

Typeset by Brighton Gray for Currency Press.
Front cover show Hannah Waterman. Cover image by Luke Stambouliah.
Cover design by Alphabet Studio.

Currency Press acknowledges the Traditional Owners of the Country on which we live and work. We pay our respects to all Aboriginal and Torres Strait Islander Elders, past and present.

NATIONAL LIBRARY OF AUSTRALIA

A catalogue record for this book is available from the National Library of Australia

Contents

The author would like to thank Margaret Woodward,
from whose story the first play, *Summer of Harold*, originated.

Summer of Harold was first produced by Ensemble Theatre, Cammeraigal Country, Kirribilli, on 8 September 2023, with the following cast:

JANET / RAE	Hannah Waterman
GARETH / JONATHAN	Berynn Schwerdt

Director, Francesca Savige
Dramaturg, Jane Fitzgerald
Set & Costume Designer, Jeremy Allen
Lighting Designer, Matt Cox
Composer & Sound Designer, Mary Rapp
Dialect Coach, Linda Nicholls-Gidley
Stage Manager, Erin Shaw
Assistant Stage Manager, Mia Kanzaki
Costume Supervisor, Renata Beslik
Lighting Secondment, Joel Montgomery

SUMMER OF HAROLD

CHARACTER

JANET, late 50s.

JANET: Three things I think of when I think of the great playwright, Harold Pinter: his cricket bat, his coffee mug, and his stained-glass window.

The window was set quite high, in a wall that faced the back garden. It featured a bat and a wicket surrounded by four cricketers, one in each panel. It must've been a wedding present, because above a garland of roses were the initials 'H-A-P'—Harold and Antonia Pinter—and the date '1980'. Under the window was a bench where Harold kept his cricket kit, giving it the look of a shrine. I remember it clearly, I passed it so often Hoovering the carpet … I should probably backtrack a bit.

1984. Fluffy fringes and lightning-bolt earrings, Phil Collins on MTV. We're nineteen, me—Janet—just out of Hobart Teacher's College and Alison from New Zealand, studying nursing. She was my housemate's cousin. We've barely met, but since we're both embarking on our great European pilgrimage, we set off together.

Our first stop is London, and we need a job. This is before the internet, remember—what backpackers do is go to this agency run by a couple of baronesses, and catering to the upper echelons of English society. We miss out on the Scottish castle job, but here's something that might be of interest: two girls to keep house for the summer in Holland Park, Australians preferred. Live-in. Sundays off. Call Mrs Pinter.

Mrs Pinter is of course the famous biographer Lady Antonia Fraser, and she asks us around for an interview. I hang up the payphone:
   'Alison, we're going to Harold Pinter's house!'
   'Who's Harold Pinter when he's at home?'
   'Who is he, you philistine? Only the most significant British playwright of the twentieth century.' (I know that because I used to go out with a drama teacher.)
   'What did he write?'
   'Heaps of stuff, loads of stuff—*The Caretaker*, completely groundbreaking.'

Blank.

'Okay, *French Lieutenant's Woman*, the movie.'

She gives Alison's shrug.

'Starring Meryl Streep? Yeah, now you're impressed. And that's just one of the hugely significant things he wrote.'

I hadn't actually seen any of his plays, but the drama teacher had some cool posters in his bedroom.

Lady Antonia is kind, gracious. Nicely put-together, as my mum would say, blonde, pearls, a twinkle in her eye. She serves Hobnobs and tea. First thing we notice is the stained-glass window, with its flannel-clad cricketers.

Harold himself stalks past, dressed skivvy to boots in black. Even his hair, black and gleaming with brilliantine. He gives us a sharp look, but leaves his wife to size us up. They have two housekeepers who go home to Spain every summer, which is when she plugs the gap with Australians: hard workers, apparently. We've already made a pact to say yes. Yes to everything. Can we drive? Yes. Can we cook? Yes! We're nineteen, we can do anything.

We turn the corner and yank off our borrowed heels, limping barefoot to the Tube in disbelief. What made *her* say yes? A pair of Antipodeans who've never cooked anything more challenging than toast, responsible for feeding the most significant British playwright of the twentieth century.

We move in on Monday.

I spend the weekend at the library boning up on his plays in case he wants to discuss them. They're really good!

We're kept pretty busy. On our first day, Lady A, as we call her, hands us her car keys to buy groceries. Yes we've driven before—in Hobart. Not in London, not to Sainsbury's in a Merc with monogrammed doors. She gives us tonight's menu and what on earth is Coronation Chicken? How the hell do you serve corned beef, roast it? (We try that, doesn't work.) We have a typed page of daily duties, everything from emptying the ashtrays and tidying the boudoir to breakfast in the fridge for next morning. Ice in the ice bucket, candles in the candlesticks.

Our room is on the fourth floor, it's called 'the nursery' and it's where we collapse at night, not so much from exhaustion but from holding our breath. Another day of getting away with it, when does it all come crashing down? We're in a constant state of semi-hysteria. It's a performance, eighteen hours a day, six days a week. But we know how to act from watching *Upstairs, Downstairs*.

She picks up the coffee mug.

Harold Pinter always uses this coffee mug. Every day, and he washes it himself. No-one else is to use it. A cup at breakfast, another mid-morning, one more after dinner. That's my job, I bring it to his study down the back of the garden. Eleven a.m., knock, leave it by the door. I'm always nervous about spilling it. Some mornings he's waiting, smoking his black Sobranie, its gold tip glinting; mostly he ignores me. One time, Lady A finds Alison making herself Bovril in it—she looks so troubled that Alison pours it down the sink.

There are a couple of other close calls.

Once, they're away for the weekend and the bathroom tap won't turn off. We're running around like Mickey Mouse in *The Sorcerer's Apprentice*, the tide creeping towards the hall carpet as we frantically search the phone book for a plumber, not so easy on a Sunday night—but luckily, Alison's Kiwi mate in Shepherd's Bush just got his licence.

Another time we collect Harold's trousers from the dry cleaner's and they've shrunk. He doesn't look happy, so I joke that he must've put on weight from our fabulous cooking. Lady A laughs, but not Harold.

And oh, yes, one day we're dusting his study. We're always cautious in there, for fear of scattering his pages or putting something back in the wrong place. Alison's gingerly wiping a sideboard full of awards, when a bee flies down her shirt. She shrieks and flings her arms out, knocking his BAFTA to the floor: it breaks! Shit shit shit shit shit. Thank God it slots back onto the pedestal. What would he have done? He wasn't scary exactly, more like … inscrutable. That's the word. You could never tell what he was thinking.

And there's the stained-glass window. We're extra careful polishing that, with its roses and ribbons and dead centre a cricket ball that, when the sun shines through, is blood red.

And so the summer progresses and nothing's gone wrong. Yet.

It's our final week in Holland Park, when Lady A comes into the kitchen to announce that next Saturday is the annual Gaieties luncheon. The Gaieties is Harold's cricket team. He's the captain, and he takes the game very seriously. In his study there's an oil painting of him in his whites; on the landing, a framed copy of WG Grace's autograph. Harold's team is made up of famous actors and playwrights, including a few 'sirs'—and they're all coming to lunch.

We're pleased with how far our culinary skills have come, and proud that Lady A thinks we can handle it. She dictates the menu. Salmon mousse, paté, ham, Coronation Chicken—again!—rice salad, watercress, French bread, fruit, cheese, and a dozen other things.

It's now that Harold appears. He says to his wife, 'Do they know how important this lunch is?'

'I'm sure they do, darling.'

He looks at us through his dark glasses: 'They'd better.' And leaves the room.

She says, 'There'll be twenty-five humans, can you manage that?' True to our pact we nod: Yes.

For the next five days, we work harder than we've ever worked in our lives. Back to the library, this time for a salmon mousse recipe. Ringing up the poulterer to see if pheasants are in season. Ordering a hare that arrives—unskinned. An expensive call home to Mum about soufflé. Vases of roses on every surface, tidying the house from top to bottom only to learn that it's in the garden, so we scrub that clean. We've got notes all over the kitchen about when to chill the white wine and how to decant the red.

And what does Alison do Friday night? Visits her Kiwi mate in Shepherd's Bush and gets absolutely rat-arsed. Wakes up in the nursery with a raging hangover.

Up to this moment, I've liked Alison. In fact at some point between roasting the corned beef and skinning the hare we've become like sisters. But right now I hate her guts.

She's chugging prairie oysters over the toilet bowl, and I'm doing everything else—folding napkins, polishing glasses and holding my breath as I lift off the mould: will our mousse be in a fish shape? Have we got enough ice? Ding dong! Bloody hell, Tom Stoppard's at the door!

'Alison, where are you? We've got to move twenty-five bowls of soup outside before they go cold!'

Alison's lying on the bathroom tiles.

Beat.

Do you know what it's like to serve twenty-five people soup, by yourself? Can't even begin to imagine? Righto, I'll show you.

The table's here. Lady A's down this end, Harold's up at that one. Along both sides you've got the cricketers, all those celebrated men of the theatre and their wives, plus a few spectators like Lady A's mother the Countess of Longford (whose best friend by the way is the Queen). Pea and ham soup, everyone! Oops, sorry Sir John, did I splash you? Of course, madam, I'll reheat it. That's just garnish, Your Lordship. More salt? There you go. Bread and butter: on its way. Too hot, madam? Well blow on it. White or Beaujolais? Let me clear your bowls. Second course!

They're onto the dessert wine when I stagger out with the lemon soufflé—oh God please don't let me drop it! … It's huge, and perfect. A beautiful day, sunshine, birdsong, everyone's having a marvellous time except Alison who finally emerges clutching her temples. They're all rather merry when Stoppard says how about a couple of practice whacks before the game? Where, *here*? Is he serious? The garden is not large and right above, there's this very beautiful stained-glass window.

The bowler actually positions himself below it. Why is nobody else concerned? I'm packing death! Harold sprints inside for his bat. This can't end well. Thanks to the cream sherry, the ball goes very wide of the mark—and over the neighbour's wall. Good, can't smash a window without a ball. Harold produces a spare! He takes his place facing the window, flexes his wrists, positions the bat as Tom winds up … and … stops. Says, 'This is ridiculous, we're too drunk.'

Thank Christ!

'We'll never hit it, let's give the Aussies a go.'

Alison turns white as he hands her the ball. I'm holding Harold's bat and facing that window. I look beseechingly at Lady A, who cheers us on: 'Bravo, girls!' There's a whole lot of jokes about the Ashes and Don Bradman that I don't understand, all I know is there's no getting out of it.

Alison limply raises the ball, we share a look like in movies where they make you shovel your own graves before shooting you.

And here it comes.

I shut my eyes and THWACK. It hurtles straight towards the window. Straight for that blood-red circle dead centre … It hits the sill, ricochets off a bench, bounces right over Gielgud's head and lands with a plop in the cream.

Howzat.

Alison beams at me with pride, but it was pure dumb luck. Amid the cheers we make for the kitchen, Lady A's calling us back. She says you must take a bow. They all applaud and we do, we bow. Then I bring Harold a black coffee—

She holds up the mug.

—he chugs it down and off they go to play cricket.

It's just us. Us and a mountain of dirty dishes. Alison raises someone's half-drunk glass of champagne: 'Here's to you, Janet. Not only did you pull it off, but you averted disaster.'

'You and me together, sis.'

They'll be hours, we've got the place to ourselves, we can lie on the carpet and play our Phil Collins cassettes and polish off the lemon soufflé. More than relieved, I'm euphoric. 'We did it!'

She flings her arms wide and drops the coffee mug: CRASH!

A horrified silence. She stares at the broken shards.

That mug, three times a day. It's not to go in the dishwasher, no-one else is to use it, the Bovril …

Of course.

The window's nothing. What mattered to him was that.

But why? You saw, it was ugly. It wasn't even very practical, the handle was too small, the rim too thick—for me anyway. Maybe that's the point, it's personal.

Perhaps it fuelled his first play and became symbolic, his future determined by a coffee mug.

Or maybe he pinched it from Judi Dench on set, that'd make it special.

Was it a souvenir from somewhere or someone he loved, someone who's gone? Did its ordinariness serve, amidst the BAFTAs and boudoirs, to remind him of the world outside? Did it mark time passing, something that remains while all around it changes?

Or maybe it just felt good to hold in his hands. The weight of it, the warmth of it.

She speaks the 'stage directions'.

Living room. Holland Park. 1984. Summer.

Janet dusting. Harold, in black, reading the paper. He looks at her, then back at the paper.

Silence.

— You're doing a good job on those knick-knacks.

— I'm glad you think so.

— I do. You lavish care on them as if they were your own.

— Thanks.

— Which of course, they're not.

— Yeah, course.

— But since you're so very careful, we have nothing to worry about.

— No. Pause. Although …

— Yes?

— I mean, if something happened, you could always get another one, right?

— Certainly, if you could go back in time. Speaking of which, is it really eight?

— Good God, and I haven't done a jot of work.

— You can take a day off now and then.

— Alright for some. You, perhaps, with nothing to contribute beyond the removal of dust from knick-knacks. When you're the most significant British playwright of the twentieth century, you can't afford days off.

— Right.

— But seeing that it *is* eight, I think I'll have my coffee.

Pause.

— Everything alright? Janet, you look pale …

Janet collapses on the rug and dies.

That was a fantasy scene, by the way. But it's playing in my head as those long hours tick by and we do the dishes in numb silence. They must've gone to the pub after the game. The clock strikes eight, the time when on any other night I'd be bringing his coffee.

Nine thirty, quarter past ten. He must know. He knows, and he's torturing us. At eleven Alison says she's going to bed, all very well for her; I'm doomed. I'm trudging up to the nursery when the front door clicks.

Deep breath.

Lady A's running her bath. But there's Harold on the sofa, eleven p.m., Holland Park, summer.

He's reading the paper.

Listen, I say, I'm afraid I've done something really terrible.

He looks up.

I broke your coffee mug.

There's a short pause, two dots rather than three, and he nods.

'Things pass through our hands. On to someone else, or gone forever. They're ours only for a moment, aren't they?'

A brief smile, then he says, 'Your soufflé, by the way, was a triumph.'

Late August. I rake the first fallen leaves from the beech tree. The Spanish ladies are due back from their holiday. Alison's meeting up with a nursing friend in Prague, and I'm off to Denmark, why not? We've pulled the toggles tight on our backpacks and helped each other hitch them onto our shoulders.

Harold and Lady A are having breakfast, and they come out to say goodbye. I feel quite emotional. I remember the morning of our interview when all of this looked so foreign: now we know the house like our own. I'm hoping I don't cry. I've got a farewell speech prepared: I'll promise to write, and should they find themselves in Launceston, there's a spare room at my parents' place. I want to tell them what a wonderful adventure it's been, and I'm wondering should I kiss them as well as give them a hug, when Harold holds out his hand. Each one says something kind, then they smile and nod towards the street—here's your taxi.

If I close my eyes I can see exactly where the spices were in the larder. I can smell Lady A's perfume, and feel the scrape of the rake on the paving. If I look around my own loungeroom now, thirty-nine years later, I realise that I've replicated the one in Holland Park: same bookshelves, fresh flowers even when I'm broke. On special occasions I make a soufflé. And when something crap happens, I remember the world's most daunting man reminding me that nothing is meant to last.

To them, we were two more in a continuum of backpackers come to cook and dust and be on our way. But to me, that summer … I take it out and burnish it.

THE END

ENFANT TERRIBLE

CHARACTERS

GARETH, late 50s.

JOANNE, late 50s.

GARETH, *in rumpled formal wear, squats staring at a small handkerchief-wrapped bundle.*

GARETH: Here it is.

I've thought about this every day. Never in my wildest dreams did I imagine it would survive the passage of time; let alone that it would come to be mine.

He unwraps it to reveal a piece of extremely old cheese.

He picks it up with reverence.

He prods it gently.

He brushes at something growing on it which, when it won't budge, he picks at carefully.

He smells it—and gags, recoiling in horror.

Who knew a piece of cheese could last thirty-nine years? Sitting on top of stereos, mantelpieces, windowsills, in the sun, becoming furred with dust. Yet here it is.

This is where everything changes, my friend. What'll I do, where'll I start? The first thing is to move out of this dump, soon as the money starts rolling in. But I'm not selling out like he did, no way. No harbourside penthouse for me, I'll go on retreat. A solo retreat, Bundanon. Japan! A year alone, no distractions, dive deep, smash through to a whole new artform. Influence the next generation, a scholarship in my name. A gallery for my work of course. I'll probably need an atelier when it becomes too much, students to do the boring bits.

And the long wait makes it all the sweeter.

Yes, but first: [*Setting an alert on his phone*] Google alerts on, Gareth Pigram …

I'm going viral, baby, hee hee!

Change.

Why tonight? What made him give it to me? Blue eyes blinking as he took my hand, placed it gently in my palm. His other hand raised to delay, for a moment, the inevitable furore.

His phone pings. He grabs it, looks, and laughs with glee.

Wheeeeee!

Leaping up, he roars and shakes his fists in the air.

Gareth, Gareth, Gareth! What the hell did you just DO?!?

He tears off his jacket and tie, does a little jig.

It'll be in the *Herald* tomorrow, all over the internet, the *enfant terrible* and his terrible act. Oh my God, my God, what inspired me? Inspired, no, I was possessed. I'm vibrating, my blood's buzzing in my veins, is this how it feels to be alive? Years of squeezing myself into the appropriate box—'appropriate', how I hate that word—choking off every natural impulse, until one night, at an awards ceremony, I burst forth. I can feel my soul expanding, I'm growing wings, what'll I do next? Ha! HA!

I wasn't even drunk. I was simply, purely, beautifully in flow. I finished, returned to the table, ate a bit more salmon. No-one moved, nobody spoke. I dabbed my lips with my napkin, looked up—and he was staring at me. With what, shock, rage, admiration? I couldn't tell.

Beat.

And then all hell breaks loose. Somebody screams, windows are flung open, two security guards are hauling me out of my chair. That's when he stops them, takes this from his pocket, still wrapped in the same ancient hanky! Too emotional to speak. Gratitude. That was it, beyond a doubt: he was thanking me for ending the charade. Well, good for him and his one remaining spark of decency.

Thirty seconds later I'm sprawled outside on my arse. Ha!

JOANNE *enters, sleepy.*

JOANNE: Darling?
GARETH: Go back to sleep.

He steers her off and shuts the bedroom door firmly.

I mean I had to do something. Three hours I'd been sitting there, smiling till my cheeks ached. First the arts minister, then the gallery director, then his manager, then Melanie his wife. Video testimonials from all over the world. Some frightful poet has written him an ode—an ode!, we endure all five minutes of that. For two weeks I'd been dreading the call, *As his oldest friend we're hoping you'll present the award?*, racking my brains for an excuse. But the call doesn't come. Neither, by the way, does an invitation, I'm not even on the guest list. I know that because I run into Melanie in the dog park.

'No? There must've been some mix-up. Of course he does, Gareth, he's just had so much on his mind. You know what he's like, brilliant at the important things, useless with the trivial. I'll put you on our table.'

The table of honour: no escape.

So there I'm stuck, grinning and nodding while the entire conversation revolves around him. *How long have you known the Great Man? Was his genius apparent from the start?*

No actually, it wasn't. Quite the opposite. Look up 'talentless', there's a photo of him. I was stunned that he even got into art school. I mean, pinch pots? Made of Das? Come on. I befriended him because I felt sorry for him, I thought, 'This poor bloke's going to be a laughing stock.' None of the other pottery students could believe it: the Bad Boy of First Year picking up this pallid, gormless worm; the guy who walked around with a rotting pig's head chained to his ankle eating lunch with a scrawny, peanut-bowl-modelling loser. But I like shocking people, always have, you can see it in my work.

He continues talking as he steps into the bathroom, leaving the door open.

An unequal friendship, sure, the host and the parasite, but a friendship nonetheless. I had a sidekick, and he had a role model. 'Where's the Valhalla, what's *Koyaanisqatsi*, can I come too?' Ditched the private-school rugby jumper and stone-wash jeans quick-smart. Winter and summer he wore this old green overcoat from the army disposal store, that always smelled wet. And he had one of those yellow cloth satchels covered in badges from bands he'd never heard, for political campaigns he didn't understand. Carried around a pipe, unlit, can you believe it? When I chose ceramic sculpture as an elective, he followed me of course. (And if he hadn't, where would the world be? No *Fountainhead* series, no *Titan's Egg*, unthinkable!) And wow, if his ashtrays were bad, his organic forms were loathsome. But the more pathetic he was, the more protective I became.

We moved into a share house in Darlinghurst.

He flushes the toilet and returns.

In second year he wasn't much fun. I don't study, barely try, yet everything I touch turns to gold. I have a natural gift whereas he, let's just say, does not.

I suppose he was resentful, holed up in the studio while I was out enjoying myself. I was the star of our year, 'the one to watch'—wore it lightly, no big deal. Let him come along to openings, introduced him to the main players. He fanboyed over all of them, I respected one or two. But the work I took seriously, so of course, he did the same.

And then one night the world was knocked off its axis, and things were never right again.

For our third-year graduation, the college holds an exhibition. The SRC turns on cask wine, some cheese and Jatz. He and I are taking photos for the newsletter. The parents come, our teachers are there. And … am I seeing things? Standing in the corner is none other than Toshiko Takaezu, the greatest living ceramicist of the twentieth century. Why's she here? Talent-scouting? Friend of the dean? What on earth is Takaezu doing at a college graduation show? Well right now she's grimacing over a polystyrene cup of wine and holding a wedge of camembert, both of which she finally dumps on the bar before disappearing into the night. Nobody else seems to have even clocked her. We turn to each other, slack-jawed. Toshiko Takaezu, people! Queen of the Clay Community! Pottery's Che Guevara!

And then he pounces. She's drained the cup, but the cheese is in one piece. He picks it up, takes out his hanky, and wraps it up like it's a butterfly wing. Carefully slides it into the pocket of his malodorous green coat.

I laugh, 'We may be starving students, but we're not that desperate.'

He stares at me: 'Eat it? This cheese has been touched by genius. I'm going to treasure it.'

Pause.

Even when he gets into his first group show in Frenchs Forest, I think nothing of it. I'm glad for him, think I even buy him a beer. And why shouldn't I feel magnanimous, I've just sold my first glazed oil burner to the guy downstairs, I'm on my way. A few months later he gets a sculpture commission. What? Really? It's for the courtyard of his old high school, hardly worth bragging about. But then he's given a residency, in Paris. I'm speechless. How is this happening? It's not only ridiculous—look at his work!—but it's profoundly wrong: he's stepped into the life that's supposed to be mine. That should be me, having French lessons. Me, throwing a farewell party where everyone draws on the walls. Me being taken to lunch by the cultural attaché. Me me me!

I stand in the doorway as he packs his bag.

'Where do I get a new housemate for six months?'

'I meant to tell you, Gareth, after Paris I'm moving in with Mel.'

Melanie. My ex. Already making a name for herself as a discerning curator. I don't care, I dumped her, if he wants my cast-offs he can go for his life.

And there's his precious little bundle, packed for travel in a Tupperware tub.

'You're not really taking that stupid piece of cheese with you?'

'Of course I am.'

'They won't let you through Customs.'

'I'll hide it.'

'Throw it in the bin, man, it's four years old.'

'I carry it everywhere.'

'Well that's just idiotic.'

'Is it? Look at what's happened to my work.'

'Your work's as hideous as ever, it's your luck that's changed.'

'You're wrong. It's my conduit to genius.'

Okay now this has gone too far.

'Listen, I saw it at the same time, I have as much right to that cheese as you.'

'But you didn't take it.'

'I didn't take it because I'm not a selfish prick!'

'No, just an envious one.'

And it's on. The one and only time we fight, and it's ugly. He accuses me of entitlement! He says, 'I'm sorry, but the Manly Art Gallery doesn't owe you a show just because you're my friend.' This, from *him*? Mr Plasticene Pinch Pot? I'm passionate by nature, I probably say some things that don't help, including a reference to his personal hygiene. But you can get over being told your breath smells like a sewer; 'entitlement'—how do you forgive a slap like that?

He leaves and we never mention it again. The decades pass, with him going from solo exhibitions to international collaborations to being the subject of a BBC documentary—where, I note, he doesn't mention his 'conduit to genius'. But it's true that he takes it everywhere, including to the presentation of a lifetime achievement award.

The award: a two-foot golden vessel draped with a fettling knife and a toggle cutter. Ghastly. The Great Man humbly approaches the podium amidst deafening cheers, shielding his eyes as if unused to the spotlight. Bows his head, palms together. Good, done, can we go home now? Oh no, it's time for the main event. Time for the Great Man to Hold Forth: his 'working-class origins', his unworthiness, standing on the shoulders of giants. Soon as his wretched drivel's over I put my shoes back on, I'm outta here. But Melanie spots me. Still embarrassed about forgetting to invite me. She hushes the applause.

'My husband's oldest friend happens to be here tonight. Gareth, would you like to say a few words?'

I glance at him, he gives a paternal nod.

Well, if you insist.

He smiles at the memory, and then bursts into laughter.

JOANNE *enters from the bedroom in her nightie, half-asleep.*

JOANNE: You're in a good mood, sweetheart.
GARETH: Go to bed.
JOANNE: How was the party?
GARETH: I'll tell you tomorrow.

He steers her off and pulls the door shut firmly.

Not just his oldest but his best friend. Might I remind you, Melanie, his best man. That's right, I had the ring. Did feel a bit odd, handing it to him to put on my girlfriend's finger— [*Acknowledging*] ex. I got sozzled before it so I don't remember much, only that he had that damned piece of cheese in his pocket. Throughout the ceremony it's all I could look at, the little sprig of handkerchief sticking out of his tux pants. I called him on it at the reception, he acted shocked, laughed at me, pulled out a normal hanky and waved it in my face. Oh yes, very slick, wasn't above a little gaslighting. But I knew, if I just waited, his time would come.

And it did. The best day of my life? No, not the birth of my first child, but the morning I opened the arts pages to a review with this heading: 'The Great Man Stumbles'. How my heart leapt! I pushed my toast aside so I could devour, undistracted, every grim word. Annoyingly, the tone was less nasty than bewildered: 'Beloved Great Man, you've let us down' kind-of-thing, 'the same soda firing he was doing in the nineties, derivative glaze-on-glaze carving', nevertheless I was ecstatic. And wait—if this, there could be others … Jumped online, searched Great Man, National Gallery, review, and YES, disappointed head-shakings abounded. I combed the net for bad crits of that show, created a file to dip into for whenever I need a boost. I dropped by his house to express my outrage, offer my condolences, and he shrugged. 'They're right, I phoned it in, too much going on. I won't let it happen again.' No indignation, no anguish—robbing me of my one and only pleasure.

The phone rings, he shuts it off without looking, obsessed now.

And he has a way of doing that, undermining you. Makes you think it's not deliberate but he's clever, I'll give him that. Rat cunning. Couple of months ago I get offered a job, a good one for a change. Teaching, yes, yawn, but for once it's not a bunch of spotty adolescents, it's a highly prestigious art school. And it pays very nicely, Joanne's over the moon because she can stop working double shifts. It's only for a term, but hey, who's complaining.

On the Monday I turn up, find my room, first class after lunch—but the door's shut. From the room emanate gasps of wonder. I've got thirty students lined up in the corridor. I peer through the glass. The classroom's full to bursting and there he is, dressed like a slob, shorts and thongs, swaggering around with his remote control, flipping through gigantic photos of himself, a clay-covered blur whirling around his studio in transports of rapture. This is my class time, I've prepared something really special. Ten minutes pass and still he dawdles at the front, chatting away, not a care in the world. Finally, out he comes.

'Gareth! I'm so thrilled!'

'About what?'

'You! Here! I'm off to Guldagergaard tomorrow.'

'You're speaking gibberish.'

'In Denmark, you don't know it? *The* major ceramic research centre.'

'So?'

'So I suggested you fill in. They wanted to go with a name, but it appears I wore them down.'

I go straight to the office and quit.

He returns to the cheese.

So what the hell was this about? It can't have been planned, he must've felt moved to respond. Because once I 'say my few words'—

He tries not to laugh.

—step down from the podium, and polish off my wine, I find his eyes on me, with that expression. Of—no, maybe it isn't gratitude. Maybe it's more like …

Hang on.

—

Was it pity?

Christ, did he misunderstand what I did up there? Does he think I've lost the plot?

No. Does he?

Oh Christ!

He patted my shoulder, eyes swimming with feeling:

—

He felt sorry for me!

'Here, old man, I've got my lifetime achievement award. For you, this sad piece of cheese from 1984. May it change your dismal fortunes.'

Don't you pity me, you hack, you fraud. Here's what I think of your pity:

He hurls the cheese across the room.

If you actually picked up the phone once in a while, if you returned my calls, then you'd know I couldn't be happier. I'm on top of the world! But you, what do you get out of life? When do you see your wife and kids? You're never home! Even if you had time to go into the studio, where's your connection with reality? Lunching with celebrities, doing press all day—how fascinating. You certainly can't be getting any work done, to call yourself an artist you have to make art.

I, on the other hand, have my freedom. I could spend entire days with my family if I actually wanted to, no fear of deadlines or Covid shutting down my retrospectives. I could work from dawn till dusk, except when I get called in to bloody teach, or Joanne gets a gig and I'm stuck with the kids. I have all the time in the world to shut the door, wedge my clay, sit at the wheel, and wait.

…

And wait.

…

And sometimes, though not often, an idea perches on my shoulder. Precious and fragile, I hardly dare glance in case it flies off. Come on, come here, coax it onto my finger, shh, let myself look.

But all I can see is you.

What would you do with it? Nothing, because it's not worth it. It's weak, pitiful, laughable. And it evaporates.

The clay dries out, and Joanne stops asking about my day.

A short silence.

I know what possessed me tonight: thirty-nine years of saying nothing. Four decades of witnessing the hypocrisy, the chicanery, the naked emperors being showered with rewards. I've been a cap-doffing withered husk, kept my mouth shut since the night he grabbed [*re: cheese*] that for himself, the moment when our paths diverged. And so when Melanie asks me to speak, what else can I do but …

A shift, as if he's witnessing himself.

… stand up, drop my napkin on the table, walk to the podium. In silence. All eyes on me. Those lights *are* actually pretty bright. And then I, do I?, no. Yes. Unzip my fly and empty my bladder, a long lazy golden arc, into the golden vessel … which is, ironically, made of metal, so it's very loud.

Zip up, sit down, tuck in my napkin.
Good God.

Beat.

Good God.

His phone pings. And again.

His uncertain smile fades. The reality of his action is sinking in, even as he resists it.

That's what I think of them and their exclusive little club, the fakers, the wankers. The Great Man droned on for forty minutes saying nothing; I said it all without a word.

Oh God.
No.
No.
It'll be in the *Herald* tomorrow, all over the internet.

He folds over, agonised, softly wailing.

His phone starts ringing, vibrating, pinging.

He runs to the bathroom, throws it down the loo. We can still hear it underwater.

He retrieves the cheese from the corner.

Took my hand and gave me this, his eyes moist. It wasn't pity. It was mirth.

He unwraps the cheese.

To me and him, a precious talisman. To the rest of the world, a prehistoric dairy product wrapped in a grubby hanky—he knew that, and couldn't resist the chance to humiliate his oldest, luckless friend. And so he gave it away, trying not to giggle. A joke.

Well fuck him.

He takes a bite of the cheese. Almost chokes with disgust but forces himself to keep going.

Fuck him.

THE END

LOOKOUT

CHARACTERS

JONATHAN, late 50s.
RAE, late 50s.

A lookout in the Blue Mountains.

Late afternoon, grey and wintry.

The sense of being at the prow of a ship, high above a vast valley.

The mist swirls, pearling everything with water droplets.

Over the course of the play, the light gradually fades to near-dark.

JONATHAN, *wearing a backpack, gingerly approaches the barrier, looks over and recoils, it's a vertiginous drop. He forces himself back to the view. He calls tentatively.*

JONATHAN: Cooee.

> *No echo.*
>
> *He tries again, a little louder.*

Cooee!

> *Behind him,* RAE *comes out of hiding and cooees loudly in his ear.*

RAE: COO-EE!!

> *He shrieks.*

Happy birthday!

JONATHAN: Oh my God.

> *She laughs.*

What are you doing here?

RAE: I followed you.

JONATHAN: Followed me? From where?

RAE: I got on the train at Strathfield and spotted you.

JONATHAN: Why didn't you say anything?

RAE: I waved but you were off in dreamland so I thought okay, I'll give him a surprise.

> *She mimics his shriek, and laughs.*

JONATHAN: Well, I'm glad you enjoyed yourself.

RAE: Happy to see me?

JONATHAN: Yeah, aside from the heart attack.

RAE: You don't look very happy.

JONATHAN: I'm still in shock.

RAE: As if I'd miss your birthday. Now stand there and let me have a look at you … Something's different.

JONATHAN: I'm exactly your age.

RAE: I don't mean you look old.

JONATHAN: I've had a haircut.

RAE: Maybe …

JONATHAN: New jumper?

RAE: Dunno. But you're still handsome as ever, darling, at least you are to me and that's what matters.

JONATHAN: Right. Thanks.

RAE: Well?

JONATHAN: Well what?

RAE: You going to tell me what we're doing here?

JONATHAN: It's our lookout.

RAE: I know that. God, I haven't thought of this place in donkey's.

She goes to the barrier, recoils at the drop.

I'd forgotten how high it is. Look at those clouds down there.

JONATHAN: I think it's mist.

RAE: Mist, cloud, whatever, you can't even see the valley.

JONATHAN: The light's fading.

RAE inhales deeply.

RAE: I'd give anything to have my sense of smell back.

JONATHAN: Smells the same.

RAE: Kind of sweet, wasn't it?

JONATHAN: Like fresh hay.

RAE: Have a big whiff for me, Jonny.

He does.

'Bring a few lungfuls back to the city', didn't we used to say that?

JONATHAN: We did.

RAE: There must've been rain, see those cascades all the way across the valley? Aren't they pretty?

JONATHAN: Yeah.

RAE: When were you last here?

JONATHAN: With you.

RAE: No!

JONATHAN: I was too upset at first; then I just forgot about it. All those Sundays I didn't come up. It's only two hours on the train.

RAE: Well I'm not surprised, I had to drag you out of bed if I remember, you complaining all the way.

JONATHAN: It was the weekend, I wanted to sleep in.

RAE: But you were glad when we got here, you thanked me then.

JONATHAN: Yep.

RAE: Which was our track?

JONATHAN: That one, from the valley.

RAE: Oh yes, you listening to your Walkman, me trying to have a conversation. By the time we climbed up here I was so puffed I couldn't talk.

JONATHAN: Always a relief.

RAE: Ha! Happy times. Just the two of us.

JONATHAN: Once I brought a friend, or tried to.

RAE: A friend? Who?

JONATHAN: Martin.

RAE: Ooh yes. Ooh no.

JONATHAN: Martin was alright.

RAE: He was after something.

JONATHAN: Like what?

RAE: I don't know, but I didn't trust him.

JONATHAN: You made him get off the train.

RAE: I did, didn't I? And you sulked all the rest of the way.

JONATHAN: He left me alone after that.

RAE: Yeah well that was the idea. God, it's all coming back. Too cold for picnics but we had them anyway, in the park, remember? Shivering in that little concrete shelter meant to look a cave.

JONATHAN: Pretty cold now, actually.

RAE: Is it? Well, whose bright idea was it to come after sunset?

JONATHAN: I didn't want to run into bushwalkers.

RAE: Why, what are you planning?

JONATHAN: What do you mean?

RAE: I hope you're not doing anything silly just because it's your birthday.

JONATHAN: No.

RAE: Bit old to start acting like a party animal.

JONATHAN: I'm not a party animal.

RAE: So what's in the bag?

JONATHAN: Nothing.

RAE: Oh no? Looks heavy.

JONATHAN *shrugs*.

JONATHAN: My stuff.

She teases him, he plays along, but when she goes for his backpack he moves it.

Just wanted the place to myself.

RAE: Am I in your way?

JONATHAN: Course not.

RAE: Good.

The moment he relaxes she grabs the backpack.

He swipes it back a little too aggressively, laughs to cover.

JONATHAN: It's funny you'd forgotten, I always think of this as your favourite spot.

RAE: Do you?

JONATHAN: Yeah.

A tense pause, broken by the sound of an incoming text. He glances at it.

RAE: Who's that?

JONATHAN: No-one.

RAE: Since when does work call you on Sundays?

JONATHAN: It's not work.

RAE: On a Sunday evening?

JONATHAN: Just a friend.

RAE: You can answer.

JONATHAN: Nothing important.

RAE: I don't mind.

JONATHAN: You used to say all those trees looked like broccoli, remember?
RAE: Call him back.
JONATHAN: Her.
RAE: It's fine.
JONATHAN: I'm with you.

Pause.

Okay I'll—

He sends a quick message, smiles to himself.

RAE: You still haven't told me, why are we here?
JONATHAN: Oh … I just started thinking about it.
RAE: What about it?
JONATHAN: You know.
RAE: No.
JONATHAN: How special it was.

She waits.

And how, you know, whatever was going on,
RAE: Where?
JONATHAN: In our lives,
RAE: Yes?
JONATHAN: … when we came up here, we were free.
RAE: Right.
JONATHAN: Didn't you feel that?
RAE: Sure.
JONATHAN: Work, school, the neighbours,
RAE: Yep.
JONATHAN: … money problems,
RAE: Plenty of those.
JONATHAN: Once you'd caught your breath you'd go straight to that railing, gaze out over the valley, and say, 'God I'd kill for a smoke right now.'

She laughs heartily.

RAE: That's not funny.
JONATHAN: Well, if you can't laugh …

RAE: I sure didn't laugh when you hid my ciggies.

JONATHAN: Our Escapade, we called it.

RAE: That's right, our special treat.

JONATHAN: It's where we were happiest. I wanted to see it again.

RAE: I've missed you.

JONATHAN: Me too.

RAE: It's been ages.

JONATHAN: Not really.

RAE: Since I saw you last.

JONATHAN: No.

RAE: Yes it has, the longest we've ever gone. You haven't noticed?

JONATHAN: Hmm.

RAE: Guess you've been busy.

JONATHAN: I guess.

RAE: What's been going on?

JONATHAN: Nothing to speak of.

RAE: But you're okay.

JONATHAN: Yeah.

RAE: You can tell me.

JONATHAN: Everything's good.

RAE: So good, you've forgotten about me.

He scoffs.

That's alright.

JONATHAN: Nonsense.

She nods at the phone.

RAE: You got a girlfriend?

JONATHAN: I wouldn't call her that.

A micro-pause.

RAE: What would you call her?

JONATHAN: I mean we're not a couple of teenagers, are we?

RAE: When did you meet her?

JONATHAN: April.

RAE: Three months ago.

JONATHAN: I suppose it must be.

RAE: It is.

JONATHAN: Gosh.

RAE: That's when I last saw you.

Which, considering how often we / used to—

JONATHAN: It doesn't feel like three months, that's for sure.

RAE: What's her name?

JONATHAN: Miriam.

RAE: That's a pretty name.

JONATHAN: Yeah.

RAE: How old is she?

JONATHAN: My age.

RAE: You can't have kids then.

JONATHAN: No, I missed that boat.

RAE: Anyway, three months, doesn't mean it's serious.

JONATHAN: I want to marry her.

RAE: —

And what does she think?

JONATHAN: We've talked about it, she's open to seeing what happens.

RAE: Very mature.

JONATHAN: I'm no good at playing it cool, you know that.

RAE: So what's her problem?

JONATHAN: She likes me, she's just a lot more experienced.

RAE: 'Experienced', hmm.

JONATHAN: Who isn't, compared to me?

RAE: I hope there isn't an ex on the scene.

JONATHAN: No, she raised her sister's three boys; then she took care of her dad but he's gone into a home.

RAE: Saint Miriam.

JONATHAN: Not at all, she's great fun.

RAE: How'd you meet?

JONATHAN: It was when I was laid up.

RAE: Laid up?

JONATHAN: Yeah I didn't tell you.

RAE: What are you talking about, were you sick? What happened?

JONATHAN: It wasn't a big deal.

RAE: Jonathan.

JONATHAN: I was hit by a cyclist.

RAE: What?

JONATHAN: On the way into work.

RAE: Jesus Christ.

JONATHAN: Look at me, I'm fine.

RAE: How can you be so calm?

JONATHAN: This is why I didn't tell you.

RAE: Did he hit you on purpose? What are you laughing at?

JONATHAN: I knew you'd think it was on purpose.

RAE: A bloody cyclist.

JONATHAN: It was an accident.

RAE: Was he on the footpath? Don't tell me it happened in traffic!

JONATHAN: I broke my leg, that's all.

RAE: Oh my God! And I suppose he took off.

JONATHAN: No she didn't. She stopped the traffic, called an ambulance—

RAE: Ambulance?

JONATHAN: Rode with me to hospital, stayed while they operated—

RAE: Operated?!

JONATHAN: And visited me until I could go home.

RAE: How'd you get up the stairs, three flights of bloody stairs?

JONATHAN: On crutches, she helped me. I couldn't go to work, or to the shops.

RAE: You had your TV dinners, thank God for those.

JONATHAN: I told her that. I tried to send her away, even showed her the freezer. She was horrified.

RAE: What's wrong with TV dinners?

JONATHAN: She couldn't believe I never learnt how to cook.

'A man of your age.'

She took a look around the flat and said where's all *your* stuff?

RAE: Why'd you let her in?

JONATHAN: I couldn't stop her, believe me I tried. She thought it was funny at first, the Corningware, the dreamcatcher, the vases of dried flowers.

RAE: Did she.

JONATHAN: She wouldn't leave until I knew how to make an omelette.

RAE: So this woman cyclist is …

JONATHAN: [*laughing*] Yes, Miriam!

RAE: Are you sure you're not her latest charity case?

JONATHAN: Pff.

RAE: Just asking the obvious. Didn't think of that, did you?

JONATHAN: She enjoys my company. I can do fish tacos now. I can do hummus, chocolate mousse. The first time she stayed over we made Bircher muesli.

RAE: I bet she was impressed with your single bed.

JONATHAN: We didn't sleep in my bed.

> RAE *reacts.*

By the time the cast came off, I was head over heels.

RAE: Well. No wonder I haven't seen you.

JONATHAN: —

—

… Actually I thought, perhaps, I didn't know if I would, again.

RAE: Would what?

JONATHAN: See you again. Because you're right, it has been a while.

RAE: I'm here now. And don't you worry, I'm not going anywhere.

Jonny, you're trembling.

JONATHAN: That wind's nippy. It'll be dark soon.

RAE: Well, it was nice to see the old place.

> *He summons his courage.*

JONATHAN: We rented a motorhome.

> *She stares at him.*

> *He giggles, nervous.*

Paid for a year in advance.

RAE: But you can't drive.

JONATHAN: I just got my Ls. For now, Miriam will drive it.

RAE: Miriam can't even ride a bike! What are you talking about, drive it where?

JONATHAN: West.

RAE: West.

JONATHAN: To start with, then we'll see.

RAE: What about your job?

JONATHAN: I quit.

RAE: No but you can't do that, you see I set it up so the bank deducts the mortgage from your salary.

JONATHAN: I sold the flat.

RAE: No. No.

JONATHAN: Gave everything to the Salvos. The Corningware, the jewellery; they didn't want the dreamcatcher.

RAE: That was my stuff.

JONATHAN: You weren't using it.

RAE: I bought that place for you!

JONATHAN: I don't want it any more.

RAE: This was her idea, wasn't it?

JONATHAN: She was going to go travelling anyway, she's sick of the rat race. I asked if I could come. You're surprised—so was she! And get this: we're throwing our phones away.

RAE: What?

JONATHAN: It's symbolic: leaving all the crap behind. We made a pact, we're really going to do it, once we pass Blackheath we throw 'em out the window.

A gleeful laugh.

I love that about her!

RAE: She sounds crazy.

JONATHAN: I withdrew ten grand.

He shows her his wallet.

Cash is good in case we end up somewhere really remote. The rest is in a joint bank account. Thirty-nine years editing *Carpet World Magazine*, it adds up. Did you ever imagine me as a grey nomad?

RAE: What's she done to you?

JONATHAN: She's picking me up at six.

RAE: Wait, slow down—

JONATHAN: In the motorhome.

RAE: —you're leaving tomorrow?

JONATHAN: Tonight.

RAE: Tonight.

JONATHAN: Six tonight. She still doesn't believe I'm coming. She said if I don't answer, it means I've chickened out and she'll go without me. No way. I'll be there.

RAE: Where's she meeting you?

JONATHAN: I don't know yet, she'll call when she gets off the freeway.
RAE: And then what? You're just—going to drive?
JONATHAN: Yeah.

> *Beat.*

I'm pretty excited.
RAE: What time is it now?
JONATHAN: Quarter to.

> RAE *nods.*

So …
> As you can see,
> I've left this till the last minute.

> *She watches him.*

> *A pause, then he takes a deep breath.*

Okay.

> *He unzips the backpack and takes out an urn.*

Obviously I couldn't give this to the Salvos.

> *She says nothing.*

Or sell it. Worth a bit, but like you said when you bought it, if I'm going to have an urn in the living room it might as well be a nice one.

> *He laughs feebly.*

> *She says nothing.*

And this was your favourite place.
RAE: Oh boy.
JONATHAN: Listen.
RAE: Oh boy oh boy oh boy oh boy oh boy.
JONATHAN: It doesn't change anything.

> *She goes to the barrier, recoils, laughs in confusion and disbelief.*

It's not like I'm going to forget you.
RAE: 'Forget' me.

JONATHAN: I'm sorry if it's a shock.

RAE: Bit of an understatement.

JONATHAN: Come on, don't be like this.

RAE: And I thought selling the flat was bad.

JONATHAN: We should've talked about it, but as I haven't seen you—

RAE: Whose fault is that?

JONATHAN: / I know.

RAE: / Not mine.

JONATHAN: / I've been preoccupied.

RAE: Preoccupied making Bircher muesli. At least you managed to spare a thought before chucking me over a cliff.

JONATHAN: Please, Mum.

RAE: Don't you 'Please Mum' me.

JONATHAN: We went over and over it, I argued, I said why can't we bring her along, she won't take up much space. But Miriam—

RAE: Right.

JONATHAN: She made me understand: [*Re: urn*] This is not you.

RAE: This woman you've known all of three months, you're letting her decide what becomes of me.

JONATHAN: But it's not you! Are you listening? It's just a container of ashes.

RAE: And how does it concern her?

JONATHAN: She can see things I don't notice, that maybe aren't that healthy.

RAE: Like what?

JONATHAN: Mum.

RAE: Like what?

JONATHAN: Okay. The first day back from hospital, she opened the front door and there was this, sitting on the coffee table. She'd only known me a week but she said, 'Now I get it.'

RAE *shrugs: 'Meaning?'*

She saw your twenty-year-old shopping list on the fridge, that you left for me; your novels on the shelf, your clothes in the closet.

RAE: What was she doing in the closet?

JONATHAN: And this, in the middle of the room.

I'd never thought about any of it, just kept on doing what we'd always done.

Beat.

She said I could only come with her if I let her go. So I made her a promise: on my birthday, I would say goodbye to you.

RAE: My darling, you've been right royally scammed. If she does a runner you you'll be lucky; what might she do to you in the middle of the desert, in the motorhome, with your wallet full of cash?

JONATHAN: Not everyone's like Ian.

RAE: I learnt my lesson and I'm begging you, please, please, to learn yours. Who'll be there to keep you safe?

JONATHAN: I don't want to be safe.

RAE: Listen to you! You had your own flat, a good job, never been in trouble, never even had your heart broken. And now you're throwing it all away?

JONATHAN: You'll still be with me, but as a memory. Not as a—

RAE: A what? What does she call me?

JONATHAN: … A force.

RAE: A force.

JONATHAN: You were protecting me, she knows that.

RAE: Right, but she doesn't care.

JONATHAN: She cares about me.

He picks up the urn.

RAE: And what happens to me?

JONATHAN: You'll merge with the elements.

RAE: Is that supposed to sound appealing?

JONATHAN: In the hospice, you regretted never having gone anywhere.

RAE: I was thinking more like Club Med.

JONATHAN: Turning into stardust and sunlight—we'll both of us be free.

She laughs bitterly.

Today as the train passed Faulconbridge, I felt sick. I called her, 'I can't do this.' She said, 'She's your mother, she'd want you to be happy.'

I've put your old CDs in the glovebox, your Slim Dusty, Chad Morgan, that stuff I used to hate, and we're going to play them all. When we stop for dinner, I'll have a curry in your honour. We'll toast you with whatever they've got to drink. And I'll tell her everything I remember, and how much I love you.

He opens the urn.

It's time.

She grabs it from him.

RAE: Jonny, you need me.

JONATHAN: I've managed without you since April.

RAE: Yes but I was still there on the coffee table—

JONATHAN: In the towel cupboard.

Beat.

RAE: In the towel cupboard; you knew that when everything fell apart you'd have me to talk to, telling you what to do. Who'll tell you what to do?

JONATHAN: I'm nearly sixty, Mum.

RAE: My little snail with no shell, too big for your age, too pale, too soft, a big freckled lump with a sign saying 'Kick Me' tattooed on your forehead. Remember when that girl from the flats across the road invited you to her pool party? Yeah? Year Seven?

JONATHAN: Don't.

RAE: All week you were so excited, 'I'm going to a party!' First five minutes they pulled off your swimmers and threw them in the barbeque. Every day, in tears after school; the TAFE was just as bad. But we had each other, didn't we? You always had me.

JONATHAN: Yes, / I know.

RAE: My first thought when I got my diagnosis was: how will he survive, how on earth is he going to survive?

JONATHAN: Surviving isn't enough.

RAE: We figured it all out together so that nothing could go wrong, and nothing has—until now.

JONATHAN: It hasn't gone wrong.

I know you think you're / helping—

RAE: What are you going to talk about?

JONATHAN: When?

RAE: On the road. Got enough material to get you past Lithgow?

JONATHAN: Sure.

RAE: Lot of time to spend with one person, especially one you barely know.

JONATHAN: We'll get to know each other.

RAE: She'll keep you entertained with her colourful past no doubt, and you? What've you done that's worth recounting? Funny stories about *Carpet World*?

JONATHAN: I've got a few stories.

RAE: Alright maybe I'm wrong, maybe she's as fabulous as you say she is.

JONATHAN: Thank you.

RAE: In which case … sweetheart, there's no nice way to say this. What's she doing with you?

JONATHAN *laughs.*

JONATHAN: Bit harsh.

RAE: Can't be your brains, obviously not your looks. I love you to bits, but I'm your mother.

JONATHAN: She likes me.

RAE: She likes you, and you're head over heels in love.

JONATHAN: She just needs time.

RAE: Time to fleece you and stomp all over your heart.

JONATHAN: Okay you've got to stop.

RAE: You're an innocent, it's the pool party all over again.

JONATHAN: No, this is different.

RAE: Is it? It's after six.

JONATHAN: She'll come.

RAE: She thinks you've got cold feet, said she'd go without you—is that someone who wants to marry you?

JONATHAN: I should call her.

RAE: She's probably halfway to Perth by now …

JONATHAN: She's stuck in traffic.

RAE: … with your motorhome and your joint bank account.

JONATHAN: You're wrong,

RAE: I don't think so.

JONATHAN: You don't know her, she's not like that.

RAE: I've heard all I need to know.

JONATHAN: I'll show you, I'll call her.

RAE: No you won't.

RAE *grabs the phone and throws it over the barrier.*

It's for the best.

He's speechless.

Darling, everything you've said to me is clear proof that you're not
yourself, you can't see what's happening, and because you've never
had to deal with people like that who are only out to use you, you
don't recognise the signs.

JONATHAN: SHUT UP.

She's stung into silence.

What've you … ?

She won't wait, I've lost her, she's gone. She's—

Oh God. Oh my God.

I don't want the flat, I don't want that job any more, I'm never
going back there again.

He throws his wallet over the barrier.

RAE: Jonny—

JONATHAN: No!

*Shocked, she watches as he takes off his shoes, then socks, and
chucks them over, followed by his clothes.*

It's what I've done my entire life: keep the door shut, don't answer
the phone, don't ask for help, don't waste your money, don't risk
it, anything could happen—but it was alright because nothing ever
did.

And now nothing ever will.

*He's down to his underwear. He stands trembling violently with
the cold.*

RAE *stares, horrified.*

She made me look forward to waking up in the morning, Mum. I
can't go back to how I was. What do I do?

He picks up the urn.

RAE: Wait.

JONATHAN: Tell me, what do I do?

RAE: Give it to me.

He clings to it.

Please.

She prises it from him, he gives up.

JONATHAN: Take good care of that, it's all I've got left. That's what you want, isn't it?

RAE: I want you to be happy.

He half-laughs, half-sobs.

Go on.

JONATHAN: Where? Go where?

RAE: Before it's too dark to see the track.

It's alright.

I'll be right behind you.

He starts to leave, when a phone rings.

It's in his hand, lit up and vibrating.

JONATHAN: Hello?

He turns back to RAE, *just as she opens the urn.*

RAE: Happy birthday.

She's about to release its contents as lights go to black.

They come up an instant later to reveal JONATHAN *in the spot where she was standing, at the barrier, fully dressed, holding the empty urn.*

THE END

SUMMER OF HAROLD

BY HILARY BELL
DIRECTED BY FRANCESCA SAVIGE
ENSEMBLE THEATRE
8 SEPTEMBER – 14 OCTOBER 2023

Ensemble Theatre proudly acknowledges the Cammeraigal people of the Eora nation as customary owners of the land on which we work and share our stories. We pay our respects to Elders past and present.

CAST

BERYNN SCHWERDT GARETH/JONATHAN
HANNAH WATERMAN JANET/RAE

CREATIVES

PLAYWRIGHT HILARY BELL
DIRECTOR FRANCESCA SAVIGE
DRAMATURG JANE FITZGERALD
SET & COSTUME DESIGNER JEREMY ALLEN
LIGHTING DESIGNER MATT COX
COMPOSER & SOUND DESIGNER MARY RAPP
DIALECT COACH LINDA NICHOLLS-GIDLEY
STAGE MANAGER ERIN SHAW
ASSISTANT STAGE MANAGER MIA KANZAKI
COSTUME SUPERVISOR RENATA BESLIK
LIGHTING SECONDMENT JOEL MONTGOMERY

RUNNING TIME 90 MINS (NO INTERVAL)
REC. AGES 14+
STRONG LANGUAGE

SUMMER OF HAROLD was commissioned by Ensemble's Literary Fund.

WINDOW, CRICKET BAT was commissioned and first produced by Griffin Theatre Company and Australian Design Centre, 11 – 21 January 2022, as a part of the exhibition Happy Objects at the Australian Design Centre.

The publication of this script was made possible by the generous support of Jenny Reynolds and Guy Reynolds AO.

Special thanks to Currency Press and Melanie Tait.

FROM ENSEMBLE THEATRE

Ensemble Theatre is the longest continuously running professional theatre company in Australia and is committed to collaborating with exceptional playwrights and creative talent to present the best international plays, modern classics and new Australian works.

It is always a fulfilling part of my job as Artistic Director commissioning a writer and setting in place the workings of a brand-new play, not only celebrated as a world premiere at Ensemble but enabling future productions by other theatre companies. With the help of our wonderful friends, Jenny and Guy Reynolds, our commissioned new work will reach wider audiences and have a brighter profile.

When I read Hilary Bell's terrific short play WINDOW, CRICKET BAT, I felt there was room to expand the idea about the curious magic of personal belongings. Thankfully, Hilary agreed, and SUMMER OF HAROLD takes this theme and populates it with rich, varied characters, dramatically poised at the points of crises. With the terrific Hannah Waterman and Berynn Schwerdt, supported by a team of talented creatives under the assured guidance of Director Francesca Savige, SUMMER OF HAROLD is a very welcome addition to the Ensemble and future Australian stages.

MARK KILMURRY, ARTISTIC DIRECTOR

DIRECTOR'S NOTE

Before our workshop of this play my mother visited. Noticing her 1980s lemon juicer on my kitchen bench, she inquired if I would care to update it. I said "No, I love this one!" Despite the hideousness of this plastic relic, I realised that it held years of memories of growing up cooking with my mum - making lemon pudding, crepes with lemon and sugar and my favourite: lemon meringue pie.

I shared this juicer revelation with the cast as we told stories of the objects that held meaning for us - a blanket, a glass cube, hand-carved bookends, a teacup. We discussed how objects can be held on to tightly or lightly, and how their significance exists only in our minds. This is the exploration of Hilary Bell's three beautiful, amusing and moving playlets comprising SUMMER OF HAROLD. Why do we cherish material things? How do they inform, infuse, infect or ignite our lives? What happens when these objects are broken or lost?

Strangely, after talking out the "juicer revelation", I felt that I could let the ugly object go now that I understood what it had meant to me. I could be free of it and still cherish those beloved hours making desserts with mum. Does telling our stories solidify our memories and release us from the material?

We have all absolutely loved working with Hilary's wonderful words and ideas, and have felt the joy of telling stories throughout the process. We hope when you read or see the play, you might afterwards find yourself sharing stories of your own objects, releasing and immortalising them.

I kept the lemon juicer.

FRANCESCA SAVIGE

WRITER'S NOTE

SUMMER OF HAROLD began as a short play, WINDOW, CRICKET BAT – a co-commission from Griffin Theatre and the Australian Design Centre for Sydney Festival 2022. Performed in the ADC's gallery space as part of their exhibition Happy Objects, it was inspired by the true adventures of Margaret Woodward, one of the contributing artists, who indeed backpacked to London in 1984 and worked as Harold Pinter's housekeeper. We nervously sent Lady Antonia Fraser the script, and her approval was relief and thrill in equal measure.

When Mark asked me to expand it for Ensemble, I jumped at the idea of diving deeper into the significance we ascribe to inanimate objects. Material things carry so much emotional weight, personal, specific, and unconnected to their function. Loaded with associations, they oppress or encourage, serve as aides de memoire or cautionary tales. These three plays, though discrete, have a thematic throughline. They speak to the ways in which a life can be shaped by an object, for good or for ill, and that recognising it for what it is can release us from its power.

Crucial to the process of this piece's development are actor Lucia Mastrantone, and Jen Rani, director of WINDOW, CRICKET BAT. I owe a debt of gratitude to them, as well as to Griffin and ADC. Also, to the artists with whom I've workshopped these plays - Francesca, Jane, Berynn, Hannah, as well as Valerie Bader and Eloise Snape, and to my clever sister Lucy Bell for her dramaturgical input. Thanks, too, to a residency in the Blue Mountains through WestWords and the Adès family (the location working its way into the final play). And of course, huge props to Ensemble for championing Australian stories.

HILARY BELL

HILARY BELL
PLAYWRIGHT

Hilary's work has been produced nationally by Griffin, STC, Ensemble, Black Swan, Sydney Opera House, Arts Centre Melbourne, Deckchair, La Boite, STCSA, City Recital Hall, NORPA, Darlinghurst Theatre Company, National Theatre of Parramatta, NIDA and Vitalstatistix; internationally by Atlantic and Steppenwolf (US) and the National Theatre (UK). Award-winning plays include WOLF LULLABY, THE FALLS, MEMMIE LE BLANC, THE RED BALLOON, ANGELA'S KITCHEN (with Paul Capsis), SPLINTER and adaptations of A CHRISTMAS CAROL, THE SEAGULL, THE COMEDY OF ERRORS and THE HYPOCHONDRIAC. She has collaborated on song cycles with composers Elena Kats-Chernin, Andrée Greenwell and Luke Styles, and musicals THE WEDDING SONG (comp. Douglas Stephen Rae, dir. Jim Sharman), STARSTRUCK THE STAGE MUSICAL written with Mitchell Butel, and with composer Greta Gertler Gold, THE RED TREE, ALL ABOARD and currently PICNIC AT HANGING ROCK. She is working with director Michael Gracey and composer Jacob Collier on a musical for UK's Scenario Two. Hilary is co-creator of best-selling picture book ALPHABETICAL SYDNEY with Antonia Pesenti, a member of 7-ON Playwrights and a graduate of the Juilliard, NIDA and AFTRS. She was the Tennessee Williams Fellow 2003-04 and the 2012 Patrick White Playwrights' Fellow at the STC.

FRANCESCA SAVIGE
DIRECTOR

Francesca holds degrees in Theatre and Acting from QUT and furthered her training in Shakespeare at RADA, Shakespeare's Globe (UK), and Shakespeare & Company (US). Frankie has pursued directing and arts education alongside her acting career since graduating. As an actor, Frankie has worked across Australia and overseas for Sport for Jove, International Actors Ensemble, Auckland Summer Shakespeare, Bell Shakespeare, Queensland Theatre Company, Critical Stages, Griffin, Parramatta Riverside, and Old Fitz as well as making screen appearances in WHEN LOVE SPRNGS (Hallmark), MARLEY, SOMEONE, THE BEEHIVE (Tribeca Short Film Festival), STARTING FROM NOW, HOME & AWAY, PACKED TO THE RAFTERS, and VENUS & ADONIS. Francesca's Directing experience includes Sport for Jove's mainstage and summer seasons as well as coordinating and directing for the Second Age Project since its inception in 2012. She has also directed for Bell Shakespeare and the renowned drama schools QUT and ACA. Most recently, she directed KILLING KATIE for Ensemble Theatre. Francesca has over 15 years' experience as a Drama and Acting teacher, working throughout Australia and internationally with individual students as well as within school and university institutions. Francesca received a 2010 Churchill Fellowship to direct and teach Shakespeare in South Africa, a 2015 Globe International Actor's Fellowship to train in London, UK, and in 2017 was a recipient of the Sandra Bates Director's Award at Ensemble Theatre to work with the company throughout the year. Frankie is a proud member of Actors Equity.

JANE FITZGERALD
DRAMATURG

Jane is Resident Dramaturg at Australian Theatre for Young People (ATYP) and was previously Literary Manager at Ensemble (shared role). Productions for Ensemble include KILLING KATIE, BLACK COCKATOO, FULLY COMMITTED and THE APPLETON LADIES' POTATO RACE. Other dramaturgy includes THE BIG DRY (Ensemble/ ATYP), CUSP, THE RESISTANCE, MROCK, SHACK, APRIL AARDVARK and BATHORY BEGINS (ATYP), SOUL TRADING (Steps and Holes, Canberra Youth Theatre) and LOST BOYS (Merrigong). For STC she has been Literary Manager and Artistic Associate as well as a dramaturg on new writers' programs and on mainstage productions. She has worked as a script reader for the Royal Court, London and worked for 15 years as a mentor with Year 12 students on HSC creative writing projects.

BERYNN SCHWERDT
GARETH/JONATHAN

Berynn has performed in more than 70 plays and musicals over the course of his career, with Sydney Theatre Company, Opera Australia, Sport for Jove and many other commercial and independent theatre companies. Musical work includes THE ROCKY HORROR SHOW, WEST SIDE STORY, SPRING AWAKENING and CERTIFIED MALE. Theatre credits include ANTONY & CLEOPATRA, LOVE'S LABOURS LOST, JULIUS CAESAR, THE IMPORTANCE OF BEING EARNEST, and THE COMPLETE WORKS OF WILLIAM SHAKESPEARE (Abridged) around Australia and in seven countries. Recent works include NORTH BY NORTHWEST, AS YOU LIKE IT and ALPHABETICAL SYDNEY. Berynn can be seen in the TV series 10 POUND POMS, and most recently played Capulet in ROMEO AND JULIET for Sport For Jove.

HANNAH WATERMAN
JANET/RAE

Training: National Youth Theatre of Great Britain.
University of Warwick, Bachelor of Arts (English
& Theatre) 1996. Theatre (Australia) MARY
POPPINS, HARRY POTTER AND THE CURSED
CHILD (Michael Cassel Group); WICKED SISTERS,
THE ALMIGHTY SOMETIMES (Griffin Theatre
Company); TALK (Sydney Theatre Company);
THE KITCHEN SINK (Ensemble Theatre); SIDE
SHOW (One Eyed Man Productions); THE WHALE
(Red Line Productions); MR STINK (CDP); LOVE
LETTERS (Hit Productions). Television: BALI 2002
(Peter Andrikidis Channel9/Stan UK Television
including but not all: EASTENDERS, THE BILL,
NEW TRICKS, THE AFTERNOON PLAY, TESS OF
THE D'URBERVILLES, TRIAL AND RETRIBUTION.
Film: MERCY ROAD (John Curran, Arclight
Pictures); PATIENT 17 (Tuyet Lee); Voice artist on
THE NIGHTINGALE (Jennifer Kent). Awards &
Nominations: Winner of the National Shakespeare
on a Platform Competition (New Globe Theatre)
1993, nominated for Best Supporting Actress
in THE ALMIGHTY SOMETIMES (GLUGS) 2018.
A proud member of Actors Equity Hannah is
delighted to be returning to The Ensemble with
Hilary Bell's stunning new play.

JEREMY ALLEN
SET & COSTUME DESIGNER

Jeremy Allen is a graduate of the NIDA Bachelor
of Dramatic Arts in Design and holds a Bachelor
of Architectural Studies from the University of
South Australia. His recent designs include: for
Sydney Theatre Company, FENCES, THE GOAT
OR, WHO IS SYLVIA set (with State Theatre
Company of South Australia), WHITE PEARL (co-
produced by National Theatre of Parramatta; for

State Theatre Company of South Australia, THE NORMAL HEART; for Griffin Theatre Company, ORANGE THROWER; for The Hayes Theatre Co., MERRILY WE ROLL ALONG set; for Red Line Productions, CLEANSED and ANGELS IN AMERICA set, 4:48 PSYCHOSIS, for Pinchgut Opera, GIUSTINO, ORONTEA, THE LOVES OF APOLLO AND DAFNE set; for Sydney Chamber Opera, FUMEBLIND ORACLE, THE DIARY OF ONE WHO DISAPPEARED.

MATT COX
LIGHTING DESIGNER

Since arriving in Sydney in 2003, Matt has designed numerous theatre productions including for Bangarra Dance Theatre: WARU JOURNEY OF THE SMALL TURTLE, DUBBOO, ONE'S COUNTRY, OUR LAND PEOPLE STORIES, BLAK, BELONG. For The Hayes Theatre Company: SHE LOVES ME. For Ensemble Theatre: BENEFACTORS, A CHRISTMAS CAROL, BOXING DAY BBQ, A VIEW FROM THE BRIDGE, A BROADCAST COUP, THE CARETAKER, NEARER THE GODS, DIPLOMACY, MURDER ON THE WIRELESS. For Bell Shakespeare: THE MISER, HAMLET, ROMEO AND JULIET. For Monkey Baa: EDWARD THE EMU, POSSUM MAGIC, THE UNKNOWN SOLDIER, DIARY OF A WOMBAT. For STC: WHARF REVUE 2020, 2019, 2018, and RUBY MOON. For William Zappa: THE ILIAD OUT LOUD. For Sport for Jove: THE LIBERTINE, OTHELLO, ANTIGONE, THE RIVER AT THE END OF THE ROAD, THE TEMPEST. For Red Line Productions: THIS MUCH IS TRUE, A VIEW FROM THE BRIDGE. For Sydney Festival: THE FAMOUS SPIEGELTENT, THE AURORA SPIEGELTENT, as well as for Carriageworks, Siren Theatre Co, the Australian Chamber Orchestra, Musica Viva and the Sydney Chamber Opera.

MARY RAPP
COMPOSER & SOUND DESIGNER

Mary Rapp (she/her) is a multidisciplinary musician, composer, and sound designer. She has a doctorate from the University of Sydney Acoustics Lab and Sydney Conservatorium of Music, comprising cross-disciplinary research in improvised music performance and acoustics science. Rapp has been commissioned to compose, design, & create sound art works for the Sydney Observatory, Haus der Kulturen der Welt Berlin, Athr Gallery Jeddah, Blush Opera Company, Noor Riyadh Art Festival, Art Gallery of NSW, NIDA, Living Room Theatre Company, and Clockfire Theatre Company to name a few. Rapp has extensive national & international performing & recording experience as a cellist, double bassist, & vocalist, in pop, jazz, classical, & art music. Rapp's performance experience includes playing with Ensemble Offspring, the Australian Art Orchestra, Courtney Act, & the Whitlams. She has played at the Sydney Festival, Melbourne International Jazz Festival, the Sydney Opera House, Memphis Orpheum, Tennessee Centre for Performing Arts, & the B.I.M. Institute in Amsterdam. Rapp teaches improvised music at the Sydney Conservatorium of Music, audio & acoustics at the University of Sydney, & music composition for screen at Macquarie University.

LINDA NICHOLLS-GIDLEY
DIALECT COACH

Linda is a well-respected Sydney based accent and dialect coach, sought after both nationally and internationally. Theatre coaching includes FADE, TINA - THE MUSICAL, MISS SAIGON, MURDER FOR 2, BENEFACTORS, CONSENT, CLYDE'S, SUDDENLY LAST SUMMER, THE ROCKY HORROR SHOW, BEAUTIFUL - THE MUSICAL,

BREAKING THE CASTLE, CINDERELLA, 9 TO 5, LET THE RIGHT ONE IN, THE CARETAKER, SLOW BOAT, PHOTOGRAPH 51, JEKYLL AND HYDE, AN AMERICAN IN PARIS, JAGGED LITTLE PILL, GIRL FROM THE NORTH COUNTRY, A CHORUS LINE, HEROES OF THE FOURTH TURNING, BLACK COCKATOO, COUNTING AND CRACKING, HOW TO TRAIN YOUR DRAGON, SHREK, SATURDAY NIGHT FEVER, THE BODYGUARD, and DIRTY DANCING. Film and Television includes SHANTARAM, WELLMANIA, YEAR OF, GORGO, MARY: THE MAKING OF A PRINCESS, THE CHASE AUSTRALIA, JUNGLE, THE HOLLOW, and VINCENT. Linda discusses accents on her podcast SAY YOU SAY ME.

ERIN SHAW
STAGE MANAGER

Erin is a graduate of the Technical Theatre and Stage Management course at NIDA. Erin has worked as a stage manager on LITTLE BORDERS and LOVE, ME for The Old 505; MOTH for ATYP; the ECHOES OF THE JAZZ AGE tour; ROMEO & JULIET for Sport for Jove; BREAKING THE CASTLE for QPAC; FOLK, DIPLOMACY (plus NSW/Vic tour), AN INTIMATE EVENING WITH PAUL CAPSIS, KENNY (plus tour), HONOUR, UNQUALIFIED 2: STILL UNQUALIFIED, PHOTOGRAPH 51, A CHRISTMAS CAROL and SUDDENLY LAST SUMMER for Ensemble Theatre, and as assistant stage manager on DIPLOMACY, THE WIDOW UNPLUGGED OR AN ACTOR DEPLOYS, BABY DOLL, THE NORMAN CONQUESTS and KILLING KATIE: CONFESSIONS OF A BOOK CLUB for Ensemble Theatre, and A ROOM OF ONE'S OWN and BLISS for Belvoir. Erin has also worked as a dresser on GIRL ASLEEP for Belvoir. Erin feels privileged to have worked with such an incredible team on this production and looks forward to the season.

MIA KANZAKI
ASSISTANT STAGE MANAGER

Mia Kanzaki is a Sydney based stage manager with a passion for diverse stories and inclusive practices in the arts. She is a recent graduate of WAAPA's Bachelor of Performing Arts (Stage Management). Her credits include BLESSED UNION, AT WHAT COST? National Tour, THE WEEKEND (Belvoir) and ASSASSINS, GLORIA and CABARET (WAAPA).

RENATA BESLIK
COSTUME DESIGNER

Renata graduated from NIDA in 2007 with a Bachelor in Costume Production. She has supervised costumes for twenty-eight shows at Ensemble Theatre with the most recent being MR BAILEY'S MINDER. Other supervising credits includes twelve operas for Pinchgut Opera most recently being MEDÉE, DARKNESS (New Theatricals), FANGIRLS (Belvoir St), BETTY BLOKK-BUSTER RE-IMAGINED (Sydney Festival), HAMLET, HENRY V, THE WINTER'S TALE, MACBETH (Bell Shakespeare), THE GOVERNMENT INSPECTOR, STAY HAPPY KEEP SMILING, THE TEMPEST, WOYCECK, A LIE OF THE MIND, PORT, THE THREESOME (NIDA). Renata is also an accomplished costume maker and milliner for films like THE GREAT GATSBY.

SUPPORT US

Every dollar counts. Ensemble relies on self-earned income to deliver all the programs that we do – commissioning new work, education outreach, producing world premieres, so please think about your capacity to make a gift to Ensemble. You can donate online at ensemble.com.au/support-us or contact Stephen Attfield, Philanthropy & Partnerships Manager, on **stephena@ensemble.com.au** or via **02 8918 3400**.

LIFE PATRONS

Those who have made significant contributions to Ensemble:

The Balnaves Foundation
Clitheroe Foundation
Jinnie & Ross Gavin
Ingrid Kaiser
Graham McConnochie
Neilson Foundation
Jenny Reynolds & Guy
    Reynolds AO
George & Diana Shirling

PLATINUM $20,000+

The Balnaves Foundation
Clitheroe Foundation
Ingrid Kaiser
Graham McConnochie
Neilson Foundation
Southern Steel Group Pty Ltd

GOLD $10,000+

Diane Balnaves
Darin Cooper Foundation
Jinnie & Ross Gavin
The James Family Charitable
    Foundation
Peter Eichhorn & Anne Willems
Philip Maxwell & Jane Tham
Steve & Julie Murphy
Victoria & Ian Pollard
Jenny Reynolds & Guy
    Reynolds AO
John & Diana Smythe
    Foundation

SILVER $5,000+

Ellen Borda
Graham Bradley AM &
    Charlene Bradley
David Z Burger Foundation

Friends of Tracey Trinder
Joanne Dan
Binu & Elsa Katari
Prue & Andrew Kennard
Mark Kilmurry & Jacqui Taffel
Peter & Marion Lean
Debbie, Garry & Val
Merryn & Rod Pearse
George & Diana Shirling
Christine Thomson
Annie & Graham Williams
Anonymous x 1

BRONZE $1,000+

The Hilmer Family Endowment
Michael Adena & Joanne Daly
Fiona Hopkins & Paul
    Bedbrook
Phil Breaden
Alexander Carmichael
Margaret Cassidy
Bill Caukill & Debby Cramer
Jayati & Bishnu Dutta
Brent & Vicki Emmett Giving
    Fund
R J Furley
Jill & Tim Golledge
Alan Gunn
Andrew & Wendy Hamlin
Matilda Hartwell
Margaret Johnston
Peter Lowry OAM &
    Dr Carolyn Lowry OAM
Michael Markiewicz
Georgie Parker
Jim & Maggie Pritchitt
Holly Stein
Bob Taffel
Wendy Trevor-Jones
The Shirley Ward Foundation
Dr Elizabeth A Watson
Gavin M. Wong

In memory of John & Vanda
    Wright
Anonymous x 3

COMMISSIONERS' CIRCLE

A group of like-minded Ensemble supporters who are passionate about storytelling and supporting artists to create new work for our stage.

Diane Balnaves
Graham Bradley AM &
    Charlene Bradley
Paul Clitheroe AM & Vicki
    Clitheroe
Jennifer Darin & Dennis
    Cooper
Ingrid Kaiser
Philip Maxwell & Jane Tham
Steve & Julie Murphy
Jenny Reynolds & Guy
    Reynolds AO
George & Diana Shirling

LEAVE A LEGACY

We would like to thank the following Estates for their generous donations:

Estate of Freddie Bluhm
Estate of Helen Gordon
Estate of Leo Mamontoff
Estate of Dimitry Nesteroff
Estate of Margaret Stenhouse

ENCORE CIRCLE

Thank you to the following people for bequests in their wills:

Mark Midwinter
Joe Sbarro
Anonymous x 6

Ensemble Theatre supporters are recognised for 12 months from the dates of donation. Current at 31 July 2023.

OUR PARTNERS

Thank you to our partners for playing a vital role in our success.

MAJOR PARTNER

THE
BALNAVES
FOUNDATION

GOVERNMENT PARTNER

NSW
GOVERNMENT

ASSOCIATE PARTNER

NEILSON
FOUNDATION

STRATEGIC PARTNER

SOUTHERN
First for Steel

SUPPORTING PARTNERS

AKCS
www.akcs.com.au

AUDIO VISUAL EVENTS

DAMN
GOOD

Hungerford Hill
ESTD 1907

KAY & HUGHES

KENNARDS
HIRE

SPS. Sydney
Physio
Solutions

ENSEMBLE ED PARTNERS

Clitheroe
Foundation

FOOD
BANK
FIGHTING HUNGER
IN AUSTRALIA

VICTORIA
AND IAN
POLLARD

TIPTOP
BAKERY

The Smith
Family
everyone's family

ENSEMBLE THEATRE TEAM

Artistic Director Mark Kilmurry
Executive Director Loretta Busby
Chief Financial Officer David Balfour Wright J.P.
Senior Producer Carly Pickard
Associate Producer Anna Williamson
Education Coordinator Alex Travers
Literary Manager Sarah Odillo Maher
Casting & Events Merran Regan
Production Manager Romy McKanna
Deputy Production Manager Paisley Williams
Resident Stage Manager Lauren Tulloh
Philanthropy & Partnerships Manager Stephen Attfield
Marketing Manager Rachael McDonnell
Deputy Marketing Manager Charlotte Burgess
Marketing Consultant David Warwick-Smith
Marketing Assistant Emma Garden
In-house Designer Cheryl Ward
Media Relations Kabuku PR
Ticketing Services Manager Spiros Hristias
Box Office Team Angus Evans, Anita Jerrentrup & Kathryn Siely
Accounts Gita Sugiyanto
Front of House Manager Jim Birch
Front of House Supervisors Megan Cribb & Isabella Wellstead
Head Chef Aurélien Girault
Sous Chef Ian Paul Aguilar Alarcon
Restaurant Manager Amy Mitchell
Maintenance Coordinator Paul Craig

ENSEMBLE LIMITED BOARD

Chair Graham Bradley AM, John Bayley, Narelle Beattie, Mark Kilmurry, Anne-Marie McGinty & James Sherrard

ENSEMBLE FOUNDATION BOARD

Chair Paul Clitheroe AM, Diane Balnaves, Graham Bradley AM, Joanne Cunningham, Ross Gavin, Emma Hodgman, Mark Kilmurry & Margo Weston

ENSEMBLE AMBASSADORS

Todd McKenney, Brian Meegan, Georgie Parker & Kate Raison

www.currency.com.au

Visit Currency Press' website now to:

- Buy your books online
- Browse through our full list of titles, from plays to screenplays, books on theatre, film and music, and more
- Choose a play for your school or amateur performance group by cast size and gender
- Obtain information about performance rights
- Find out about theatre productions and other performing arts news across Australia
- For students, read our study guides
- For teachers, access syllabus and other relevant information
- Sign up for our email newsletter

The performing arts publisher

www.ingramcontent.com/pod-product-compliance
Lightning Source LLC
Chambersburg PA
CBHW050024090426
42734CB00021B/3408